Little Acorn

and the Great Big Happy Hug

Nurturing interactive story and activities

Hilary Hawkes

Strawberry Jam Books

"Together may we give our children

roots to grow and wings to fly" Anon.

Hello from Story Therapy® (part of Strawberry Jam Books).
We're a small, not-for-profits/voluntary project and member of Social
Enterprise UK. Our resources aim to promote inclusion, friendship and
understanding of ourselves and others. Our products are available to all,
but we also donate our books and resources to groups, registered
charities and organizations that help children's emotional growth and
mental well-being. www.hilaryhawkes.co.uk/strawberryjambooks

Words © Hilary Hawkes

Front Cover:Pushkin /shutterstock.com according to license agreement and tree on template: pixabay.com

Back cover and inside illustrations as follows: Snail, worm, leaves, bird, butterfly, roots, grass with daisies, leaf buds, sapling tree, badger, chicks, squirrel, owls, frogs and acorn: credited to Pixabay.com. Cartoon forest landscape and beneath the soil image: MSSA/shutterstock.com, Rainy sunny day: Galyna Puzyrna/shutterstock.com – all according to their licence usage agreements. Title page background: katarinochka/Thinkstock. Page leaf border background: 100kers/istock/Getty images

First edition by Strawberry Jam Books 2016

British Library Cataloguing in Publication Data

A CIP catalogue record for this book is available from the British Library

Strawberry Jam Books

Abingdon-on-Thames, UK

www.hilaryhawkes.co.uk/strawberryjambooks

ISBN Ebook 978-1910257-227 Print 978-1910257-23-4

Little Acorn and the Great Big Happy Hug

This story is part of the award winning Story Therapy® series from Strawberry Jam Books, created by author Hilary Hawkes.

See www.hilaryhawkes.co.uk/strawberryjambooks for details & titles

This is a story about security and love and all things that enable our children (and little acorns) to thrive.

Suggestion: First: share the story together, looking at the pictures. Next, read the story again and invite your child/children to imagine they are Little Acorn slowly growing into a strong tree.

Look out for Snippy Snail in each picture of the little acorn story!

He looks like this:

Deep in the woods, under the fallen leaves and the soft soil, lies one brown baby acorn. It is warm and still and sleepy.

Imagine you are a baby acorn! You are curled up: still, warm and peaceful in the soil.

Down in the soil
it is snuggly safe,
dim and dark
and calm and cosy.

Little Acorn feels
warm and
peaceful
and happy.
The soil is tucked all around…
Like a great big happy hug.

Crrrrrrr…….rack!

Imagine a little root has popped out of your acorn shell. It wiggles and wriggles further down into the soil.

The soil is good and your root drinks in the goodness.

And the goodness makes you feel…good!

A shoot begins to grow out of the top of
your acorn shell
and s l o w l y wiggles and wobbles and
jiggles and joggles its way upwards.
Your arm can be the wiggly growing
shoot as you move it above your head.

You see a teeny, tiny glint of light through the soft soil above.

Your shoot makes its way upwards to the teeny tiny glint of light.

Up

Up

Up it goes!

And further up! Until...

…it bursts through the soil into the dazzling daylight!

Slowly stand or stretch upwards! Your little shoot feels the warmth of the soothing sun.

It feels good.

Gentle spits and spots of rain fall.

Soon you have become a new baby tree called a sapling.

The warmth and the rain and the light
feel like *a great big happy hug*.
As a sapling you begin to grow tougher
and taller and faster and fatter and
strong and **sturdy**!
A butterfly and a bird sit gently in your
new gently swaying baby branches.
They are your new friends.

The goodness from the light and the warmth and the rain go down, down, down to your root.

Imagine that under the ground, in the soil, your root has grown bigger and bolder and stronger and longer too.

Another root grows. And then another. And another!

Stretch out your arms and stand tall!

Time goes by and Little Acorn grows and grows and grows.

You are no longer just Little Acorn or a new sapling!

You are Little Oak.

High up in the sky the bright sun shines and smiles down at you. And the sun's smile feels like *a great big happy hug*.

You stretch out your branches even more until…POP!

Leaf buds appear on your branches!

Wispy white clouds blow across the sky.

Then more gentle rain falls.

You like the rain.

Nearby Big Oak looks down at you and rustles its big leaves and its strong branches.

"Well, look at you! You're wonderful!" it says.

This makes you feel all smiley, warm and safe.

The sun and the rain, your friends sitting in your branches and Big Oak's words are like *a great big happy hug*. And so you grow big and strong and happy!

The End.

Have fun with the next story activities too! Story activities and games can help children relax and calm down and develop their imaginations. They

step back, be calm and reflective.

Little Butterfly

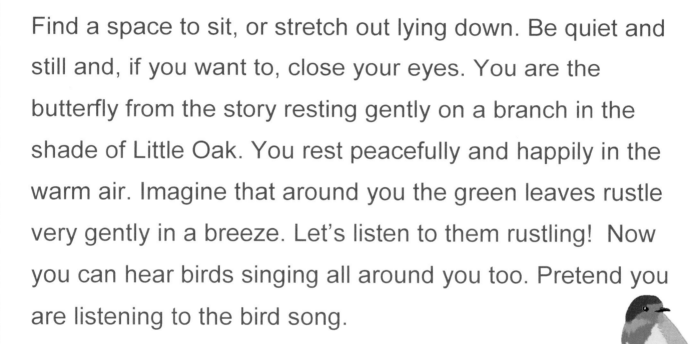

Imagine you are a butterfly!

Find a space to sit, or stretch out lying down. Be quiet and still and, if you want to, close your eyes. You are the butterfly from the story resting gently on a branch in the shade of Little Oak. You rest peacefully and happily in the warm air. Imagine that around you the green leaves rustle very gently in a breeze. Let's listen to them rustling! Now you can hear birds singing all around you too. Pretend you are listening to the bird song.

The birds sound cheerful and happy. You feel happy too, and content in the safe branches of the tree. Now have a little stretch and, if you had your eyes closed, open them.

If you were sitting or lying down then slowly and carefully stand up.

Butterflies love to fly. Slowly and carefully stretch and open your arms to your sides. Pretend your arms are your butterfly wings. They can be red or blue or yellow or pink or whatever you imagine. Think about your wings. Very slowly and gently move your wings up and down. Stretch upwards or stand on tip-toe if you can. Imagine flying upwards just a little way. You can look down at the branch and the leaves.

Now move slowly and carefully to another spot on the floor. Move your wings gently up and down as you fly. Then, in your new place carefully and slowly sit down again. Now imagine you are you again.

Rest your arms by your sides or place your hands in your lap or on your knees. Pretend you are sitting beside Little Oak tree watching the butterfly and listening to the leaves rustling and the bird song. Take a slow breath in and out and feel calm and peaceful.

The Owl

Let's imagine a big owl comes to visit Little Oak in the woods!

Find a place to stand tall and straight.

You are the big strong wise owl. You sit high up in the branches of Little Oak. Your big magnificent wings are folded by your side. Give your arms a gentle shake. Pretend your arms are your big strong owl wings. And now be still again.

Above you the night sky twinkles with bright stars. Look up at the stars. It is calm and quiet in the night-time woods.

Now it is time to stretch out your huge wings. Stretch your arms out sideways. Now slowly, slowly -  imagine you are the owl leaving the branch to fly up above the trees.

Fly slowly and carefully around. You are a wise and important owl looking for the next place to land.

You can soar upwards, higher towards the sky and the stars and the moon. You feel free and happy as you fly.

Now you drop downwards towards another tree branch. Find a place to stop and slowly sit down. You have carefully landed on another branch. You fold your wings against your sides again.

Take a slow deep breath in and

a slow deep breath out.

Sit tall and proud and magnificent

as you wait quietly on your strong branch.

Be glad to be you!

I AM HAPPY

I AM GLAD TO BE ME

I AM STRONG

I AM PEACEFUL

I AM BRAVE

I AM LOVED

Little Acorn grew into a healthy and happy tree! Sometimes, you might not feel happy, but there is a part of you inside – the real you – that can begin to feel calm and peaceful again anytime.

For grown-ups:

Find the picture affirmation cards on the Story Therapy® page of Strawberry Jam Books website * where you can download them, print them out onto card and then cut them to make a set of cards. Get children to think about the things that make them feel calm, brave, happy etc. You could write those things on the back of the cards if you want to.

Talk together about how remembering these things can help you feel strong or calm. Encourage children to look at the cards anytime and especially at times when they might feel sad or unhappy.

* www.hilaryhawkes.co.uk/strawberryjambooks/storytherapy

Other books and resources you may like in the Story Therapy® series:

Imagine!

Cd or audio download

Eight fun, calming, interactive narratives with music– join in or listen and imagine! Children's meditation/relaxation activity included. Includes Little Acorn and The Great Big Happy Hug. Narrated by Sharon Hoyland.

Stories for Feelings for Children

Paperback, audio or ebook

Illustrated and non-illustrated versions

Seven nurturing stories that help children with feelings and emotions. Themes include loss, change, anxiety, believing in yourself etc.

Just Be with Bizzy Bee!

Print and ebook

Fun story with rhyming and relaxation activity.

The Forever Tree

Print

Fun interactive story – imagine you are the Forever Tree – standing firm through all the seasons. How to deal with worries and anxieties tips at the end of the story.

See www.hilaryhawkes.co.u/strawberryjambooks